FIRED UP!

Making Pottery
in Ancient Times

FIRED UP!

Making Pottery in Ancient Times

by Rivka Gonen

Runestone Press • Minneapolis

RUNESTONE PRESS • RUNESTONE

rune (rōōn) *n* **1 a :** one of the earliest written alphabets used in northern Europe, dating back to A.D. 200; **b :** an alphabet character believed to have magic powers; **c :** a charm; **d :** an Old Norse or Finnish poem. **2 :** a poem or incantation of mysterious significance, often carved in stone.

Thanks to Dr. Guy Gibbon, Department of Anthropology, University of Minnesota, for his help in preparing this book.

Words in **bold** type are listed in a glossary that starts on page 68.

Library of Congress Cataloging–in–Publication Data
Gonen, Rivka
  Fired Up!: making pottery in ancient times/ by Rivka Gonen.
    p. cm—(Buried Worlds)
  Includes index.
  Summary: Discusses how pottery was made and used in ancient times and describes how archaeologists use these vessels today to learn about the past.
    ISBN 0–8225–3202–6 (lib. bdg.) 1. Pottery—Juvenile literature. [1. Pottery] I. Title. II. Series.
CC79.5.P6G66 1993
738.3'82—dc20   92–41748
                                                              CIP
                                                              AC

Manufactured in the United States of America
1 2 3 4 5 6 – I/JR – 98 97 96 95 94 93

CONTENTS

1 Picking Up the Pieces 6

2 Making Pottery 18

3 Designs, Decorations, and Finishes 36

4 Pottery in the Ancient World 50

5 Reading the Pottery Record 58

Pronunciation Guide 68

Glossary 68

Index 70

PICKING UP THE PIECES

Thousands of years ago, before humans learned to make things from metal, glass, or plastic, most containers were made from clay. Clay is a fine-grained soil that can be easily shaped when wet. Ancient people worked lumps of clay into shapes, let them dry, and then baked them in hot fires. This baking process—called **firing**—transformed the soft clay into hard pottery.

Pottery is just one aspect of a craft called **ceramics.** Ceramic objects include bricks, drainpipes, tiles, beads, jewelry, plates, pots, and ornaments. The term *pottery* usually describes clay containers.

Archaeologists—scientists who excavate (dig up) and study objects from the past—examine pottery to understand how ancient people lived. Because fired clay does not rot, ancient pottery, including broken pieces called **potsherds**, is often scattered across excavation sites.

Archaeologists can piece together these potsherds and can learn how the restored **artifact** was used in ancient times. Decorations on potsherds can even tell archaeologists if an object was a storage container, a cooking pot, or some other clay product.

Pottery can also help archaeologists to determine who lived on a particular site. Different peoples had different ways of making and decorating pottery. In addition,

An early Greek amphora (a two-handled storage vessel) leans against stone ruins on Delos, a Greek island in the Aegean Sea.

pottery styles changed from one period of history to another. For this reason, pottery can help archaeologists to **date** (determine the age of) ancient sites.

The ancient methods of pottery making are still in use. Much modern pottery, however, is manufactured on a large scale. Machines shape the clay, which is then fired in gigantic ovens at very high temperatures. The resulting products range from simple household items to valuable works of art.

The First Pottery

Although prehistoric humans appeared hundreds of thousands of years ago, pottery was not developed until much later. The earliest peoples probably used other materials to fashion the containers they

Restorers can often fit together pieces of pottery (below)—*called potsherds—to reconstruct a broken vessel* (right).

Prehistoric humans probably made the first baskets from tall grasses and leaves. These early containers later served as models—and possibly as molds—for early pottery.

needed for storing, cooking, and carrying things. Archaeologists believe that humans first made bags out of the skins of animals, hollowed out gourds for bowls, carved dishes of wood, and wove baskets from plant fibers.

Humans started firing pottery between 10,000 and 12,000 years ago, but they had been shaping clay for more than 100,000 years. Archaeologists have found evidence that people who lived before the invention of pottery had already developed many of the methods used in making pottery itself.

Prehistoric people knew how to prepare a soupy coating—called

These unbaked clay figures are about 10,000 years old. Thousands of years before humans learned how to fire (bake) clay, they shaped this material into decorative and useful objects.

slip—to hold clay pieces together and to decorate a pot's surface. They also knew how to **burnish** (polish) clay surfaces. They used these techniques to make designs on the clay floors and walls of their houses. In addition, they painted and decorated clay figurines. But true pottery was not invented until people learned that fire could permanently harden clay.

Archaeologists believe that hunters and gatherers were also wanderers who wanted to carry strong, light objects rather than heavy pottery. Durable clay objects began

The early inhabitants of North America probably used simple pots for saving seeds and for cooking their food.

Discovered in north central Japan, this jōmon pot is decorated with sculpted figures of roosters and dragonflies.

THE JŌMON OF JAPAN

Early inhabitants of Japan made the world's oldest known pottery —called *jōmon* (meaning ''rope-patterned''). Named for this style, the ancient Jōmon people were hunters and gatherers who lived in Japan as early as 10,000 B.C.

Jōmon craftspeople built the walls of their pots with many long coils of clay. After smoothing the sides of a vessel, potters pressed twisted ropes into the pot's exterior. This technique gave the surface an intricate lined pattern.

Jōmon potters fired their wares at low temperatures, which made the pots porous. To prevent liquids from seeping out, artisans often painted their pots with ocher—a yellow or reddish-brown soil mixed with oil.

By about 3500 B.C., the Jōmon had started making a new style of pottery called flaming jōmon. Originating in north central Japan, flaming jōmon pots were decorated along the rims with sculpted forms of animals and other figures. By studying the shapes of the jōmon vessels, as well as their decoration, archaeologists have learned a great deal about how the ancient Jōmon people lived and worked.

An archaeologist—a scientist who finds and studies ancient objects—catalogs a collection of ancient pottery found in Costa Rica, a Central American country.

to replace leather bags, wooden bowls, and woven baskets when people started to settle down and build more permanent villages.

Although archaeologists are not certain how early people learned to fire clay pots, they have found some clues to this puzzle. Excavators discovered that ancient people built their cooking fires in shallow, clay-coated holes. The cooking fires hardened the clay and transformed it into a pottery basin set in the ground. This hardened clay may have given prehistoric people the idea to fire other clay objects.

Archaeologists have also found potsherds marked with the im-

Archaeologists believe that early humans, while using shallow, clay-coated pits to prepare food, discovered that fire permanently hardens clay.

pressions of woven baskets. They believe ancient people may have coated the insides of their baskets with clay. When a coated basket fell into a fire, the basket fibers burned to ashes, but the clay on the inside hardened.

The discovery of pottery occurred in several different places at different times. Pottery appeared in the Middle East around 7,000 B.C., in China before 5,000 B.C., and in the Americas by about 5,000 B.C.

The Ancient Potters

The first potters were probably women, who made dishes, cook-ware, and other household items. This tradition continues, especially in many African and Native American societies. In rural Mexico, for example, women are considered the most skilled potters. They perform every aspect of the craft from digging the clay and constructing the pots to gathering the fuel used to fire their artwork.

In ancient times, pottery making eventually changed from a household task to a full-time profession. Merchants sold pottery as durable storage containers for goods that traveled by land and sea. As trade increased, pottery became an industry, and more and more men became potters.

A traditional Japanese potter shapes small bowls. Archaeologists believe that the Japanese were the first people to fire clay.

BURIED BEAKERS

Throughout Europe, archaeologists have unearthed pots shaped like inverted bells. Scholars have named the people that made these pots the Beaker folk and their culture is often called the Bell-Beaker culture. Archaeologists believe that the Beaker folk, who lived about 6,000 years ago, probably originated in Spain and migrated to central and western Europe on raiding missions.

The Beaker folk were warlike people who made weapons—such as spears and arrows—from bronze, a metal made of copper and tin. In fact, their search for copper deposits helped spread the knowledge of metalworking across the European continent.

Because they moved from place to place, the Beaker folk left no traces of settlement. Their graves, however, held ceremonial goods, including weapons and pottery. The Beaker folk decorated their bell-shaped pottery in several ways. Some potters pressed rope into the exteriors of their pots. Other artisans imprinted designs with fine-toothed combs or with spiked wheels. These techniques were most often used to create patterns of evenly spaced, horizontal bands.

Many archaeologists believe that beaker pottery was related to social status. For this reason, some scholars study this distinctive pottery, as well as weapons and other grave goods, to learn how the Beaker folk organized their culture.

The Beaker folk, who lived in western and central Europe as much as 6,000 years ago, crafted bell-shaped drinking cups decorated with geometric designs. Archaeologists found this example in Wales, which is part of the United Kingdom.

Potters set up workshops to produce large quantities of containers. As certain shaping and firing techniques became standard, the styles of pottery became more uniform. Some craftspeople became traveling potters who moved from village to village, making pottery wherever they could find work.

The craft that had begun as a household task eventually became one of the most important

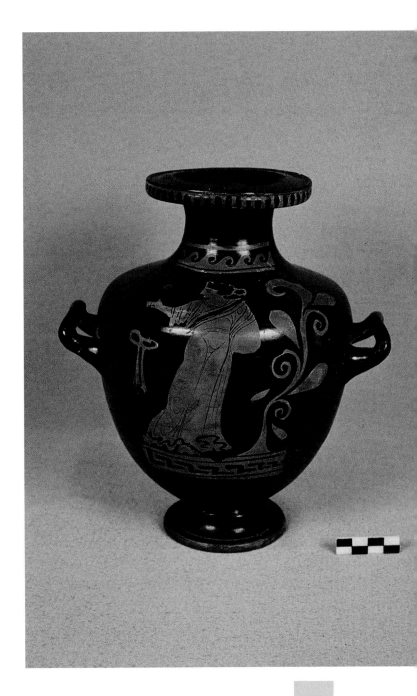

Ancient Greek potters crafted black- and rust-colored vessels that were valued for their intricate design.

Using slip—a soupy mixture of clay and water—a Native American woman smooths the inside of a pot. Women, because they needed to make cookware and household items, were probably the first potters.

industries of ancient times. Many potters were highly respected artisans. In fact, the potters of ancient Greece took such pride in their distinct styles that they signed their pots.

Some potters formed partnerships with artists, who decorated the finished pots. Archaeologists have uncovered pottery signed by both the potter and the artist—discoveries that highlight the importance of this art form in ancient times.

Ancient potters often set up large workshops to produce everyday containers, as well as more valuable pieces traded as artwork.

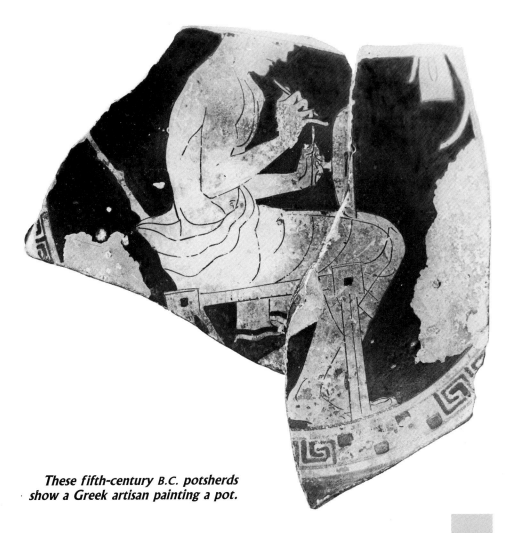

These fifth-century B.C. potsherds show a Greek artisan painting a pot.

MAKING POTTERY

Natural forces, such as wind, rain, and sun, break down hard rock into sand, silt, and clay particles to make earth. When wind and water move dirt from one area to another, clay particles can be left behind in concentrated **deposits.**

Types of Clay

The size of individual clay particles—called grains—determines how workable the clay will be. Fine grains stick together easily when moist, allowing the clay to be made into many different shapes without falling apart. As a rule, the finer the grains, the more easily the clay can be molded.

The purest form of clay—known as **kaolin**—is made of the fine, white crystals of feldspar, a very

hard mineral. When fired at very high temperatures, kaolin becomes **porcelain.** The finest and most delicate-looking pottery, porcelain is both transluscent (able to let light through) and durable. It is often called **china** because it was first made in China.

The Chinese used fine kaolin as a coating material—or **glaze**—for clay vessels by 1500 B.C. In about A.D. 600, larger deposits of kaolin and better methods of firing allowed the Chinese to produce their famous porcelain. For centuries, the Chinese made and exported the world's finest porcelain.

Most clay, unlike kaolin, is mixed with other minerals. The minerals change the color of the clay to hues that range from yellow to a deep reddish brown. Firing these natural,

Workers use tractors (below) to dig up large amounts of clay, including kaolin (right)—a fine-grained, white clay.

19

This Chinese porcelain vase is made of kaolin. Kaolin hardens into porcelain—a strong, translucent ware—when fired at very high temperatures.

mixed clays at lower temperatures produces **earthenware,** which is porous (allows liquid through). Earthenware can be made waterproof by glazing. When the same clay is fired at higher temperatures, however, it becomes **stoneware,** which is nonporous.

Preparing the Clay

Potters cannot use clay exactly as it comes out of the ground. Clay must be treated to make it easier to work with and to ensure that the finished product will be strong after firing.

Clods of clay are dug from the earth and ground into powder so that the clay will mix properly. Clay workers remove stones and pebbles by putting the material through a sieve or by mixing the clay with water so that large, heavy particles sink. If the clay does not mold easily enough, finer clay has to be added. In other cases, the clay might mold

Traditional potters sometimes use shallow refining pools to help prepare their clay. As the clay soaks, coarse particles sink to the bottom, leaving only the fine grains to be worked into pottery.

so easily that it will not hold its shape. In this instance, potters add coarser ingredients to stiffen the clay.

After the clay is mixed to the right consistency, materials—such as sand, gravel, chopped straw, or groundup potsherds—may be added. These materials create spaces for air in the dense clay.

The air spaces allow the clay to breathe and let water evaporate from the clay more easily. Without these materials, the clay might dry unevenly or crack. Potters then knead the clay to make it soft and

A potter carefully kneads a lump of clay to remove air bubbles, which can cause a pot to crack during firing.

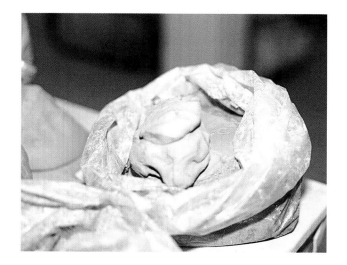

This clay, which is soft and moist, is ready for use.

smooth and to eliminate air bubbles, which could cause breaks or flaws in the clay during firing.

Although clay is ready to be used at this point, most experienced potters prefer to store the clay and let it age. As clay ages, each particle becomes thoroughly and evenly moistened, making the material more workable. Traditional Japanese potters sometimes aged their clay for an entire generation—

A potter smooths the inside of a hand-built pot.

Using the coiling method, a potter rolls a lump of clay into a long strip. The potter will make many of these coils to build the walls of the pot.

about 25 or 30 years—before passing it on to their children.

Shaping by Hand

The simplest method of working with clay is to hold a lump in the palm of one hand and to shape it with the other. This method is called **hand building** and was probably the first technique used by ancient potters. The easiest hand-building method consists of pinching the clay into a desired shape. Modern sculptors, who often mold a form from a lump of clay, use a hand-building method called solid forming.

While small bowls and cups are easily formed by hand building, large, complicated shapes are more easily made with **coil construction.** Using this method, a potter forms a flat piece of clay that will become the base of a pot. The potter then rolls long, thin strips that look like clay snakes. These long shapes are coiled along the top of the base.

By laying one strip on top of the other, the potter builds the walls of the pot. The potter can widen or narrow the pot by making the coils larger or smaller. Potters use slip to hold the coils together and to smooth the inside, and sometimes the outside, of a coil-constructed pot.

Ancient potters also used the slab method, which consists of pounding clay into flat slabs. Using one slab as the base, the potter attaches other slabs with slip to form the walls of a pot. Because large slabs can be difficult to work with, pot-ters often let them harden slightly before joining them together.

Pottery from Molds

Another very old technique of pottery making is the use of **molds**—objects that give their own shape to the soft clay. The mold method is used to make identical pieces of pottery. The potter simply flattens a lump of clay into the shape of a pancake. The lump is pressed into

A potter cuts a thick slab of clay, which will form one side of a vessel.

The craftspeople of Arretium (now Arezzo, Italy) crafted the famous Arretine ware from molds that gave the pottery uniform and detailed designs.

the inside or onto the outside of the mold to copy the mold's shape.

The earliest molds were probably vessels, such as baskets, gourds, or leather bags. The Pueblo Indians in the southwestern United States, for example, formed the lower part of a clay pot inside a hollow gourd and then finished the upper part with coil construction.

The mold method has two distinct advantages over coil and slab construction. Molding is faster and permits the potter to make many pots with the same carved or stamped decoration. Between 30 B.C. and A.D. 30, ancient Roman potters in the city of Arretium (now Arezzo, Italy) produced vessels with

Roman soldiers carrying shields and swords decorate this ancient, molded oil lamp.

25

molded decorations. Known as Arretine ware, this famous molded pottery carried geometric shapes and images of plants, animals, and people.

Molds were used to make a variety of objects. In ancient times, the most common molded items were oil lamps and small statuettes used for religious purposes. Sometimes artisans molded decorations to attach to the pottery's surface.

The Potter's Wheel

Ancient potters who used coil construction usually worked on a movable surface, such as a piece of wood, a stone, or a woven mat. By turning the work surface, the potter could sit in one spot and shape all sides of the pot evenly. The practice of using movable work surfaces goes back to very early stages of pottery making and may have provided the original idea for the potter's wheel.

The potter's wheel, however, was quite different from other movable work surfaces. It turned at a much greater speed, building up centrifugal force that tended to throw the clay outward from the center. The potter carefully controlled the clay by keeping it exactly in the center of the wheel and by forcing it into the desired shape. This process,

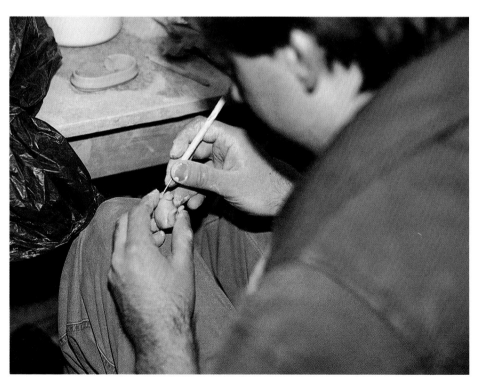

Potters often use molds or small tools to shape decorations for their pots.

An artisan on the Mediterranean island of Cyprus forms a water jug on a manually operated wheel.

which modern potters still use, is called **throwing.**

As long ago as 3500 B.C., a kind of primitive turntable was used in making pottery. Ancient potters rotated small pots on these turntables, probably to make the sides smooth after they were formed by some other method. Archaeologists are certain that this turntable did not spin fast enough to throw a pot.

The earliest true potter's wheels were found in the ruins of Ur (in modern Iraq), one of the oldest

Archaeologists uncovered this stone potter's wheel, which dates to about 1300 B.C., at the ancient site of Hazor in Israel. With a cone-shaped spindle pointed upward from its center, the flat surface of the bottom disk (left) rested on the ground. Using the center hole, potters fitted the top disk (right) on the spindle.

known cities in the world. Each of these ancient wheels consisted of two round disks of stone or baked clay. One disk rested on the ground and had a short spindle sticking out of its center. The second disk, which had a hole in the center, was mounted on the spindle.

Archaeologists believe that early potters fastened a larger disk of wood over the top disk, allowing a helper to spin the wooden disk

This model of an ancient Egyptian workshop shows a potter shaping a bowl as an apprentice turns a hand wheel.

while the potter shaped a pot. This type of potter's wheel was used for thousands of years, until the invention of the foot-powered wheel.

The foot wheel, much like the early potter's wheel, consisted of a revolving disk mounted on a spindle. The potter or a helper pressed pedals, which operated a system of pulleys that turned the wheel. This type of wheel was a great step forward, since the potter could use

Like the ancient potter's wheel, the modern wheel, which can be powered electrically or manually, consists of a revolving disk mounted on a spindle.

Using an electric wheel, artisans press a floor pedal to turn the disk of the wheel.

This potter turns a foot-powered wheel by moving a kick bar back and forth.

both hands for forming a pot. Modern wheels are often powered by a small electrical motor, which turns the wheel when the potter presses a floor pedal.

The use of the potter's wheel originated in the Middle East in about 4000 B.C. and spread gradually to India, China, and Japan in the east and to the Mediterranean region and Europe in the west and northwest. The potter's wheel did not completely replace the old methods of hand building or coil construction.

For example, the people of Cyprus—an island in the eastern Mediterranean Sea—began using

Until the 1500s, when Europeans introduced the potter's wheel, craftspeople in the Americas shaped pottery by hand. The Maya of Central America hand crafted simple jars with detailed paintings (right). *The Anasazi Indians from what is now the southwestern United States made pottery with intricate geometric designs* (below).

the potter's wheel in 2000 B.C. to produce their everyday household pottery. At the same time, however, they continued to make a very beautiful hand-built pottery that was exported all over the Middle East.

In the Americas, the potter's wheel was unknown before the arrival of Europeans in the sixteenth century. Until the 1500s, the great civilizations of Central America and South America made magnificent hand-built pottery.

Archaeologists unearthed this hand-made jug in Cyprus.

Painted with several colors of slip, this Nazca jar displays the features of a human face.

THE NAZCA CULTURE

The Nazca culture thrived in the South American country of Peru from 200 B.C. to A.D. 600. The people of this region farmed fertile land, which supported corn, squash, beans, and other crops. Because the Nazca were strongly tied to the land, they worshiped fertility figures. They represented these deities on their pottery as humans, animals, birds, fish, seeds, and plants.

The Nazca crafted their pottery in simple shapes. Early Nazca wares consisted mostly of bowls and double-spouted jars with flat handles. Later Nazca potters created many vessel forms, including jars that are shaped like human figures.

The Nazca decorated their pottery in many shades of brightly colored slip. Potters usually painted the backgrounds white or red. Designs were outlined in black and filled in with a variety of hues, mainly red, orange, brown, and purple. Artisans used bold lines to paint angular figures. These characteristics of color and design have made this unique pottery a Nazca trademark.

Ancient African potters combined hand building and coil construction to make pots shaped in the form of human faces.

Combined Methods

Many ancient potters used a combination of pottery methods. Around 2000 B.C., for example, the ancient Syrians typically used both coil construction and the potter's wheel. They made the bottom halves of their pots with coils and formed the neck and rim on a wheel. The two halves were joined, and the joint was disguised with patterns of lines scratched into the surface.

Archaeologists are uncertain why the potters of ancient Syria used this method. Their fairly advanced wheels produced fine necks and rims but could also have turned fast enough to produce the bottom halves. Even small vessels, which easily could have been made entirely on the potter's wheel, were constructed in this combined fashion.

Archaeologists speculate that in Syrian workshops pottery making was divided between workers. The less skilled laborer might have used coils to build the body of the pot, while the master potter would throw the necks and rims on the wheel. Many traditional potters in the Middle East and in the Mediterranean still produce pots in this manner.

After using a wheel to shape the bottom half of his pot, a modern potter carefully constructs the top half with coils (above) *to create a uniform shape* (right).

DESIGNS, DECORATIONS, AND FINISHES

The first potters had little difficulty in finding shapes for their pottery. They simply copied the designs of early containers, such as gourds, reed baskets, wooden bowls, and leather bags. Some ancient potters used these objects to directly transmit their shapes to the pottery.

Artisans often decorated their pottery in an effort to copy the shape and appearance of familiar objects. They used paint to create the look of wood or stone or scratched lines into clay surfaces to imitate the weaving of basketry or the stitching of leather bags.

Clay—unlike wood, stone, gourds, basketry fibers, and leather—can assume almost any shape. Pottery can be made in oval, rectangular, or round forms. For thousands of years, artisans have created clay containers in these forms, as well as in the more complicated shapes of animals and humans.

Techniques of Decoration

A wide range of styles was used to decorate ancient pottery. Potters could cut, stamp, or comb various

Dating to about A.D. 400, this ancient, hand-built pot from the South American country of Peru, appears in the shape of a human.

Ancient potters often copied the shape or the design of other containers. The surface of this ancient beaker is scratched with a basketlike pattern.

decorations into soft clay. With clay, they added figures and designs to surfaces. Potters also cut designs into surfaces by removing clay.

Potters could cut holes of any shape or cut away entire sections of their pots. In addition, artisans applied paint, slip, or glaze to surfaces. Modern potters continue to use many of these ancient methods.

Different groups of people favored different designs at different periods of time, offering archaeologists clues to when and where certain groups lived. Painting was the most common method of decorating pottery in ancient times.

Prehistoric artists used four basic colors. They made black paint from charcoal and white hues from kaolin. Red and yellow paint came from animal blood and from ground iron, a silver-white metal that rusts in moist air. By 2000 B.C., ancient peoples had learned to make many other colors by combining natural minerals found in the ground.

Ancient potters painted a variety of designs on their pots, from simple geometric lines to complicated landscapes and scenes of people and animals. Archaeologists value these paintings for their portrayals of life in ancient times.

In some cases, pottery images are the only surviving artwork from certain cultures. For example, in the ancient Mediterranean and Middle East, artisans often decorated the plaster walls of buildings with paintings called **frescoes**. In some of these regions, not a single fresco has survived, but the pottery paintings that remain have given archaeologists some idea of how the frescoes might have looked.

The Uses of Slip

Slip is a thin mixture of clay and water that potters often use to give a clay surface uniform texture and color. Slip is applied before firing, either by brushing it on or by dipping clay objects in the mixture. Slip adds color and gives pottery a smooth surface.

The difference in color between the clay of the pot and the clay of the slip is sometimes used to create

Crafted in about 1500 B.C., this painted vase was discovered on Crete, a Greek island in the eastern Mediterranean Sea.

interesting decorations. Potters can paint slip on some parts of pots, while leaving the rest in the original color. Or they can apply slip to the entire pot and then scratch through the slip to reveal the clay underneath. The techniques of working with slip can become quite complex, but they can result in beautiful designs.

In Athens, the capital of modern Greece, archaeologists uncovered elaborate fired pots, dating to the fifth and sixth centuries B.C. These pots featured black- and rust-colored decorations of humans and animals.

Originally, archaeologists thought the colors were paint. Laboratory analysis of the pottery, however, has established that both the black

A pottery student uses slip to smooth the surface of a recently thrown pot.

Ancient Greek potters applied slip to this pot—which is called calyx-krater—to create its elaborate black- and rust-colored designs.

and rust colors were made with the same slip and that this slip contained no paint pigment. The secret of the ancient Greek potters was not in their use of pigment but in their methods of applying the slip and of firing the finished vessel.

Ancient Greek potters, like modern potters, fired their clay in ovens called **kilns.** When a kiln is left open during the firing process, air containing oxygen moves freely over the pottery. This allows slip to return to its original color—usually

Diggers found this ancient burnished (polished) pot in Peru.

put rust-and-black designs on the same piece of pottery. To achieve these colors, they painted parts of their pottery with very thin coatings of slip and other portions with very thick coatings. They then fired the pottery in an open kiln, and the entire piece took on a rust color. Then the kiln was closed, and the pot was fired again until the piece turned black. When slightly opened again, the kiln let in just enough oxygen to turn the thin coating of slip back to rust. This method resulted in designs in rust and black.

rust or red. When a kiln is closed no oxygen flows into the oven, and the slip turns a glossy black.

Some ancient potters used their knowledge of the firing process to

Burnishing and Glazing

Before firing a clay object, ancient potters often rubbed the surface

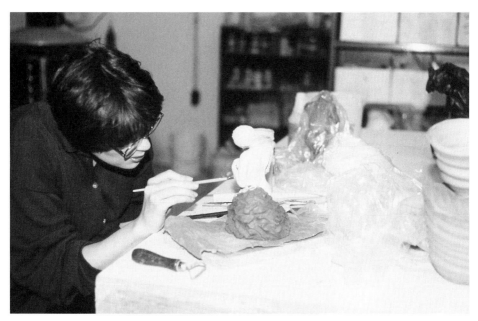

A potter puts a thin layer of glaze—a glossy, waterproof coating—on a clay sculpture.

Thousands of clay warriors stand at the entrance to the tomb of China's first emperor, Qin Shihuangdi.

CHINA'S CLAY ARMY

In 1974 workers digging a well near the city of Xi'an in east central China dug up some buried pottery. Their find led to the discovery of a three-acre (1.23-hectacre) underground vault located near the tomb of China's first emperor, Qin Shihuangdi. The vault contained an army of about 8,000 life-size clay warriors, complete with horses and war chariots.

Qin Shihuangdi ordered the building of his vast tomb in 247 B.C. Archaeologists believe that artists crafted the clay soldiers to protect the emperor during his journey into the afterlife. Each soldier bears a different face, which scholars believe might have been modeled after actual people.

The figures are made of terracotta, a hard earthenware. Terracotta ranges in color from tan to dark brown to various shades of red. The clay used to make terracotta is easy to mold and is very durable after firing. In fact, many of the warriors look much as they did when they were buried more than 2,000 years ago.

Decorated with glazes of many different colors, this Chinese bowl dates to about 300 B.C.

with a stone, a piece of wood, or some other hard material. When the pot was fired, these rubbed areas turned smooth. This process—called burnishing—is still used by modern potters. Burnishing brings particles of clay closer together and improves a pot's ability to hold water. Potters usually burnish pots that have been coated with slip, a technique that gives pottery a fine, glossy finish. One of the oldest decorating methods, burnishing was widely used by the early inhabitants of the Americas.

Glaze, another type of surface decoration that originated in ancient times, is a thin, glossy material that makes pottery waterproof. Although composed of the same basic material as clay, glaze includes ground glass and minerals and melts at lower temperatures. After firing, a glazed pot looks shiny, as if it has been dipped in glass. In fact, the word *glaze* comes from an old English word for glass.

The people of Mesopotamia, a region in southwestern Asia, invented the first glazes in about 4000 B.C. This early glaze consisted of powdered copper ore that craftspeople melted onto small objects, such as beads. By about 2000 B.C., the Mesopotamians learned to make glaze that could be easily worked when heated to a liquid. The technique quickly spread to nearby civilizations.

The ancient Egyptians mixed powdered quartz—a clear rock— with natron, a mineral containing sodium that is found in the western deserts of Egypt. Potters either combined this mixture with copper to create a rich turquoise color or with another mineral called manganese to make a deep purple. Eventually, they also learned to produce glazes in brilliant hues of blue, black, red, and yellow.

Pottery made with these glazes is called **faience.** Although this glazing technique was invented by the Egyptians, it is named after the Italian city of Faenza, which is famous for a similar type of pottery.

The sodium-based faience glazes were used by potters throughout the Middle East and the Mediterranean. But powdered, lead-based glazes, which were easier to prepare and apply, were more common in ancient times.

Ancient potters mixed a variety of minerals to create brightly colored glazes, such as this turquoise hue, which contains copper.

Lead glazes were probably invented in the Middle East in about 2000 B.C., when potters discovered that minerals containing lead melt quite easily. Potters could simply sprinkle lead glazes evenly over damp clay. When fired, the glaze melted to a beautiful finish. Potters could also combine lead glazes with other minerals, creating the same brilliant colors produced by faience glazes.

Into the Fire

After a potter has crafted a pot and has decided on finishing decorations, the pot must be hardened in the firing kiln. Firing tests the skill of the potter. Air bubbles that have not been kneaded out can cause flaws. Faulty joints between the strips of a coil-constructed pot will become visible. A pot that is not dry enough before firing may even

A potter carefully builds the brick walls of a firing kiln.

The opening of this traditional stone kiln will be sealed with mud to prevent heat from escaping. Most modern kilns are made of brick or metal.

explode in the kiln, ruining other pots that are being fired with it.

Potters must always let a finished clay pot dry before it can be fired. As the clay object loses water, it begins to shrink. By the time the object is ready to be fired, it will have decreased in size by about 10 percent. If the pot is not dried slowly and evenly, it may warp and crack as it shrinks in the high temperatures of a kiln. When it is almost completely dry, the pot is ready for firing. At this stage a pot is extremely delicate. It will shatter if dropped or disintegrate if put in water.

Clay loses its last traces of water as it is fired. On average, by the time a kiln heats up to about 600° F (318° C), the clay has completely dried. When the temperature reaches about 850° F (458° C), clay hardens permanently. Different types of clay, however, harden at different temperatures.

A group of Pueblo potters in New Mexico bakes its artwork in the flames of a wood-burning fire.

Some large manufacturers of pottery use computer-controlled kilns.

The oldest potsherds uncovered by archaeologists are black earthenware, indicating that the earliest pottery may have been fired in open bonfires. An open fire can produce temperatures as high as 1300° F (710° C), which are hot enough to fire most earthenware objects. Smoke from the fire turned much of this early pottery black.

The uneven heat of an open fire probably cracked many ancient pots. The earliest pottery was also so porous that it probably could not hold liquid. Early inhabitants may have solved this problem by coating their pottery with animal fat. In time, prehistoric potters began using more advanced firing techniques. In fact, some prehistoric pottery looks as if it was fired in a kiln, but archaeologists have not found any kiln remains that prove this theory.

The oldest known kiln was discovered in Palestine (present-day Israel and Jordan). Dating to about 3000 B.C., the kiln was a round structure with two chambers, one above the other. Ancient potters built a fire in the lower chamber, and the heat of the fire flowed through large holes into the upper chamber, which held the pots to be fired.

Such kilns could generate temperatures as high as 1600° F (878° C)—hot enough to successfully fire any earthenware clay. Potters throughout Asia and the Mediterranean eventually used this type of kiln.

An artisan removes his pot from a dome-shaped kiln.

POTTERY IN THE ANCIENT WORLD

Pottery played a very important role in the lives of ancient peoples, who used pots for cooking, for eating, and for storing their supplies. Traders shipped wine, grain, and other goods in pottery containers. Artisans made fine, intricately decorated pottery and sold their wares to admirers.

Household Pottery

At the ancient site of Hazor, Israel, archaeologists unearthed two homes that date to about 800 B.C. Although much of the pottery that excavators found was in the form of potsherds, archaeologists were able to piece together many of the broken vessels. From this evidence, and from pottery found in many other ruins, archaeologists have been able to form a picture of how a typical ancient family might have used pottery.

The most common dishes at Hazor were bowls. Because excavators found no plates or cups, archaeologists believe that ancient families ate and drank mainly from bowls. Cooking pots, all of similar shape, were made of hard, coarse clay that was blackened with soot. To cook their food, Hazor's inhabitants built fires in pottery stoves. They covered the stoves with upside-down pots to heat their food.

Excavators also found several deep, two-handled bowls among

the ruins at Hazor. Since these bowls were not blackened on the outside, they probably were used only for mixing foods. A variety of jugs used for serving liquids were unearthed, including one that was shaped like a modern canteen.

Large pottery basins were probably used for washing.

Excavators also dug up numerous storage jars from this site. The largest jars stood about 30 inches (76 centimeters) tall, while smaller jars were about 18 inches (46 cm)

This round, wide-mouthed container—called a krater—probably served as a mixing bowl in ancient times.

Dating to about 1100 B.C., this collection of pottery includes vessels with pointed bases. Archaeologists believe that these containers probably held wine or water and were leaned against walls for storage.

high. All of the jars had two handles and pointed bases, but they differed in shape. The bases prevented the jars from standing on their own. Therefore, the jars were kept in small depressions in the dirt floor and were leaned against the walls of the house.

Archaeologists unearthed few oil lamps. The lamps they did find were very simple, consisting only of a bowl, which once held flammable oil and a wick. The lack of oil lamps suggests that the inhabitants of Hazor went to sleep at dusk and rose at dawn.

Containers for Trade

In many cases, pottery has been unearthed at sites far from where it was originally made. From this discovery, archaeologists have concluded that pottery was widely traded. Some of this pottery was exported from regions that specialized in a certain style of fine pottery. Most vessels, however, were simply used as containers for products that were being transported.

Plain, undecorated pottery vessels that could be closed with a lid or a cork probably carried the three most important products of ancient times. In the Middle East and the

The shapes of ancient trading vessels often imitated the goods they carried. This pot's shape resembles the seedpod of a poppy—a plant from which the drug opium is made. The shape may have warned traders and merchants that the container held a dangerous substance.

Archaeologists in Israel discovered this large storage vessel in pieces and restored it to its original shape.

Mediterranean, these exports were grain, wine, and olive oil—products that did not spoil easily and could withstand long journeys by land or sea.

Archaeologists believe that, because few people could read or write in ancient times, labels were rarely used to identify the contents of trading vessels. Instead, some pottery was formed in shapes associated with the goods they held.

For example, jugs for carrying opium—a drug used as an ancient painkiller—were shaped like the seedpod of the poppy plant, from which opium is made. The shape of the opium jar was used to identify the dangerous drug.

The Finest Pottery

Some of the pottery that was widely traded in ancient times was not designed to contain goods. This pottery was shipped to other countries simply because it was finely made. Wealthy buyers treasured these vessels as works of art.

One example of the fine pottery trade comes from the ancient

The Etruscans, who lived in northwestern Italy between 650 B.C. and 450 B.C., crafted a shiny black pottery called bucchero. Bucchero artworks were widely traded for their beauty.

The early inhabitants of South America traded finely made pots with painted designs. This pot was unearthed on the northern coast of Peru.

GREEK SHAPES

Although ancient Greek artisans are well known for their beautifully designed and decorated vases, most Greek pots were made for everyday use. Potters crafted many types of dishes and storage containers, all of which had distinct shapes.

For example, wine—a valuable commodity in ancient times—was mixed with water and served at most meals. For this reason, common pottery included wide-mouthed wine jars, water jars, bowls for mixing, jugs for pouring, and cups for drinking. Oils and perfumes, on the other hand, were kept in narrow-necked flasks.

When archaeologists discover potsherds (fragments), they divide them into closed (narrow-mouthed) pot styles and open (wide-mouthed) pot styles. Potsherds from closed pots are usually rough and unpainted on one side, while fragments from open pots are smooth and sometimes decorated on both sides.

Archaeologists have given special names to the shapes of Greek pots, which evolved over time. The *hydria,* for instance is a closed pot with a rounded body and a short, narrow neck. The *stamnos,* an open pot, looks much like the hydria but its neck is shorter and wider. Scholars have assigned names to the styles of nearly every Greek pot, each of which had a particular role in everyday life. By identifying the shapes of excavated pots, archaeologists can determine how Greek pottery was used at a certain place and time.

This Greek vase, which probably held wine or oil, is called an amphora.

In the ancient town of Ostia, Italy, an artist depicted a sailor loading goods for trade on this mosaic, a picture created from small pieces of stone set in cement. Ancient potters made tall, oval-shaped pots to carry grain, wine, and olive oil—three valuable commodities in the Mediterranean region.

Greeks. Considered expert potters, the Greeks began exporting their rust-and-black, slip-decorated pottery in the seventh century B.C. In the sixth century B.C., potters from Athens learned the technique of painting black figures on pottery. This superior pottery was in great demand throughout the Middle East and the Mediterranean. As a result, Athens dominated the pottery trade for several hundred years.

Greek vases, oil jugs, bowls, cups, and vessels were shipped from Athens to ports in Egypt and Syria, where they were unloaded and sorted into smaller shipments. Traders on camels and mules transported the smaller loads overland to wealthy cities in Asia, Europe, and the Middle East. Archaeologists have found fine Greek pottery in the ruins of almost every ancient Middle Eastern and Mediterranean settlement.

READING THE POTTERY RECORD

One important aspect of archaeology is determining the age of unearthed remains. By studying the time period in which artifacts were made, archaeologists can sometimes learn about the history and culture of an ancient settlement. Archaeologists use two methods to find the age of an object—**absolute dating** and **relative dating.**

Absolute dating determines the approximate year that an object was made or used. Relative dating places objects in a time sequence by determining which artifacts were used earlier and which came later.

For example, if we say that the airplane was invented in about 1900, we are giving an absolute date. On the other hand, if we say that the airplane was invented after the steam engine and before the television, we are giving a relative date. Pottery is important to the processes of relative and absolute dating.

Relative Dating

Over the years, settlements are covered by many layers of earth called **strata.** In ancient times, when garbage collectors did not exist, people simply tossed their trash into the streets. Pressed into the dirt of hard-packed roads, the garbage became part of a very thick stratum.

Pottery, which is one of the most common finds on ancient sites, is often buried in layers of earth called strata. A recorder *(below)* charts layers that have been identified and labeled. An excavator *(right)* carefully brushes dirt from an ancient pot.

Eventually, however, events occurred that disrupted the lives of the settlements' inhabitants. Perhaps war broke out, or invaders appeared, or a volcano erupted. Sickness and famine often caused ancient people to abandon their settlements. These disasters often deposited their own stratum of material, such as ashes, dust, or the rubble of ruined buildings.

Over time, new styles of pottery were developed by ancient potters or introduced by foreign invaders. The broken remains of this pottery were added to the street garbage.

As strata grew, these different styles of pottery were left embedded within the various layers. As a result, archaeologists generally find early pottery styles in bottom layers of strata and later styles toward the top.

By carefully recording the location of each pottery artifact, archaeologists can arrange their finds in order from the very oldest to the most recent. This process is called **sequence dating.** After comparing sequences from many different ruins, archaeologists have been able to establish systems of relative

Archaeologists sometimes find artifacts that offer clues to how ancient peoples lived and worked. This early Egyptian wall painting shows potters mixing clay and shaping pots.

The British archaeologist Flinders Petrie grouped ancient pottery by shape and style and assigned each group an approximate date. This method, which is called sequence dating, helps archaeologists identify their finds.

dating for almost every type of ancient pottery.

The British archaeologist Flinders Petrie recognized the importance of pottery in the process of dating. He developed the technique of sequence dating in the late 1800s.

Petrie unearthed many ancient graves in Egypt. Since a grave is used only once, Petrie realized that all artifacts found in a tomb would date to the same time period. Unlike the strata of a ruined settlement, graves are not found on top of one another. Each grave is dug in a different place, and the depth at which each is found does not indicate its age. Petrie was faced with vast quantities of pottery and no way to tell which styles were the oldest and which were developed later.

Petrie put similar styles together and sorted the pottery into several groups. He noticed that wavy handles on the Egyptian pottery showed small changes in style from one group to the next. He arranged

Some early potters decorated their work with royal names or symbols. This potsherd is marked with the symbol of an ancient Egyptian king.

the groups in a sequence from the plainest handles—which he thought were the oldest—to the most elaborate handles, which may have been made more recently. Petrie's guess was eventually confirmed by other evidence.

Petrie developed a similar system of sequence dating for pottery found in Israel and Jordan. In this case, however, he had the advantage of referring to the stratum in which each pottery artifact was found. Petrie's techniques have become the standard methods used in relative dating.

Absolute Dating

If ancient potters had written the date of manufacture on their pottery, archaeologists could just pick up an ancient vessel and find an absolute date with no further effort. Potters did not date their work, but they often wrote the names of rulers on their pots. By knowing the dates of rulers' reigns, archaeologists can determine absolute dates. Pottery can also be given an absolute date if it is found together with date-stamped coins or in a building carved with the date of construction.

Archaeologists can sometimes use Egyptian pottery to date distant sites in the Middle East, Asia, and Europe. Because the Egyptians developed an early writing system and kept dated records of their ancient rulers, the absolute dates of their ancient pottery are well established. When archaeologists discover an Egyptian-style pot in a certain site, they can then date a collection of objects or an entire stratum of the site.

The Egyptian king Akhenaton, who came to the throne in 1379 B.C., provided archaeologists with a highly accurate dating method. Akhenaton moved the capital of Egypt to a new city named Tell al-Amarna. Seventeen years into his rule, Akhenaton died, and the new capital was abandoned. Thus, everything found in the ruins of Tell al-Amarna dates from this 17-year period.

Mycenaean III/A, a type of pottery made in Mycenae (now part of Greece), was used in Tell al-Amarna. This particular type of pottery has also been unearthed in Israel, Jordan, Syria, and Cyprus. Wherever Mycenaean III/A pottery is found, archaeologists know that it belongs to the Tell al-Amarna period and can date all other objects on the site to that time.

Laboratory Dating

In recent years, archaeologists have also used advanced laboratory methods to determine the age of an ancient artifact. Although archaeologists consider the results of these methods as absolute dates, the years are only approximate.

The most common laboratory method is **radiocarbon dating.** This technique relies on the fact that living organisms contain not only ordinary carbon but also small quantities of radioactive carbon, commonly called carbon-14.

Radioactivity occurs when the central mass of an atom breaks up and produces energy. Organisms (all living things) absorb carbon through food or air. When alive, organisms have about the same amount of carbon-14 as they have of ordinary carbon. When an organism dies, it no longer absorbs either type of carbon. Instead, the radioactive carbon-14 gradually loses its radiation and becomes ordinary carbon. This shift in the ratio of carbon to carbon-14 takes place at a known rate.

Scientists test an artifact made from organic matter to determine exactly how much carbon-14 remains. If most of the carbon-14 is still there, the object cannot be very old. If, on the other hand, the carbon-14 is nearly gone, the living organism that the object was made of must be very old. Its age can be measured in years, and an approximate date can be found.

Radiocarbon dating can be used on any object made of a once-living substance, such as wood, paper, leather, bone, reeds, or cloth. Since it was never alive, pottery cannot be dated with this method. When these once-living materials are found near pottery, however, the pottery itself can be given an absolute date.

To determine the age of fired clay, lab workers use **thermo-luminescence dating.** All clay stores energy from natural radioac-tivity. When clay is heated above a critical temperature of 752° F to 932° F (400° C to 500° C), this radiation is released in the form of light. The light, which is invisible, can be seen with special instruments in a laboratory. When potters originally fired their pots, all the energy, or thermo-luminescence, was released. After firing, the pottery began to store radiation again at a measurable rate.

Scientists can determine the amount of absorbed radiation by firing a piece of pottery under carefully controlled conditions. The amount of light released during the firing process indicates how much time has passed since the pottery was last fired or—in other words—how old the pottery is.

With the help of a computer a laboratory worker records and analyzes carbon-dating results.

Scientists using the carbon-dating method need glass vacuum systems *(right)* to convert organic (once living) matter to the chemical benzene. Scintillation counters *(below)* use benzene to detect the amount of carbon-14, a material that decays at a known rate.

Many modern potters still choose traditional methods to make household wares, as well as beautiful works of art.

Companies that make pottery have created new equipment, such as this fast-firing kiln, to mass-produce dishes and other items.

Thermo-luminescence dating is not very accurate. In fact, the dates this method gives may be as much as 15 percent in error. But the method can still give a rough idea of the age of a pottery object. Museums often use thermo-luminescence to determine if a piece of pottery is ancient or a forgery.

The Pottery Tradition

The ancient tradition of pottery making continues to be passed on from one generation of potters to the next. Modern potters still make everyday items, such as dishes, cooking pots, and containers. They also create works of art that stand next to the pottery of ancient artisans in museums around the world.

Pottery is not only useful and often beautiful to look at but also reveals information about the lives of past civilizations. In the future, archaeologists will be able to look at contemporary pottery and learn as much about our time as today's archaeologists have learned about the time of the earliest potters.

Discovered in Cyprus, this amphora dates to the sixth century B.C.

PRONUNCIATION GUIDE

Arretine (AHR-uh-teen)

bucchero (BOO-kuh-roh)

faience (fay-AHNTS)

Jomon (JOH-mohn)

kaolin (KAY-uh-luhn)

Maya (MY-uh)

porcelain (POHR-suh-luhn)

GLOSSARY

absolute dating: to determine the approximate year in which an object was made or used.

archaeologist: a scientist who studies the material remains of past human life.

artifact: any object made by a human. Artifacts can include items crafted from natural materials, such as bone, stone, clay, or wood.

burnish: to shine a clay surface by rubbing it with a hard, smooth object before firing.

ceramic: any object made of clay that is baked at high temperatures. Pottery is a specific type of ceramic that includes only containers.

china: a fine kind of porcelain that originated in China.

coil construction: a method of building the walls of a pot with rolled strips of clay piled on top of one another.

date: to determine the era in which an object was made.

deposit: materials—such as sand, clay, or minerals—that wind or water have carried to an area.

earthenware: pottery that is fired at low temperatures. Earthenware is slightly porous (filled with tiny holes through which air and liquid can pass).

faience: a type of earthenware containing minerals that produce brilliant colors when fired. Although the Egyptians invented faience, it is named after the Italian city of Faenza.

firing: the process of baking clay at high temperatures to make pottery.

fresco: a painting made on wet plaster with water-based paints.

glaze: a hard, glasslike coating melted onto the surface of pottery during the firing process. Glazes come in many different colors.

hand building: a method of making pottery by forming clay into a desired shape with the hands.

kaolin: a fine-grained white clay used for making porcelain.

kiln: a special kind of oven used by potters to bake clay.

mold: an object that shapes soft clay. Molds allow potters to make many containers with the same shape and decoration.

porcelain: a hard, white earthenware made from kaolin clay. Pottery made of porcelain is often called china.

potsherd: a piece of broken pottery. Potsherds are common on archaeological sites.

radiocarbon dating: a method of dating ancient objects by measuring the amount of radioactive carbon—called carbon-14—that remains in a once-living material, such as wood or leather.

relative dating: the process of determining the order in which objects were made without regard to their actual age.

A potter prepares clay for throwing.

sequence dating: a method of determining the order in which different versions of a certain object were made or used over a long span of time.

slip: a thin mixture of clay and water used to smooth clay surfaces or to create designs.

stoneware: clay objects that are fired at high temperatures. Stoneware is nonporous (does not contain tiny openings through which air or liquid can pass).

stratum: a separate layer of earth or sediment on an archaeological site that may contain ancient artifacts or human remains.

throw: to form a pot on a potter's wheel.

thermo-luminescence dating: a method of dating based on the fact that certain materials in pottery store radioactive energy over time. This energy, which is released as light, can be measured precisely in a laboratory.

INDEX

Absolute dating, 58, 62–63
Africa, 13, 33–34
Akhenaton, 63
Anasazi Indians, 31
Archaeology, 9, 27–28, 32, 35, 38–39, 49, 52
  dating methods, 8, 58–67
  excavations, 6, 12, 50–51, 59–60
Arretine ware, 25–26
Arretium (Arezzo), 25–26
Athens, 40, 57

Beaker folk, 14
Bucchero, 55
Burnishing, 10, 42, 44
Central America, 12, 31–32
Ceramics, 6
China, 13, 18, 20, 30, 33, 43–44
Clay, 6, 8–10, 12, 18–35, 36, 38, 47
  deposits, 18
  preparing, 20–23
  types of, 18–20
Coil construction, 11, 23–26, 34–35
Containers, 8–10, 13, 15, 17, 36, 53–54
Cyprus, 27, 30, 32, 63
Dating, 8, 58–67

Decorations, 6, 10, 17, 25–26, 31, 36–49
Designs, 10, 15, 17, 31, 34, 36–49
Earthenware, 20, 49
Egypt, 44–45, 57, 60–63
Etruscans, 55
Europe, 30–31, 57, 63
Excavations, 6, 12, 50–51, 59–60
Faience, 45
Firing, 6, 8–9, 12, 18, 20–22, 40–42, 46–49, 64, 67
Frescoes, 38–39
Glaze, 18, 20, 42, 44–46

A street vendor in Iran sells water jars.

An experienced potter guides a child through the process of throwing a pot.

Greece, 7, 15, 17, 33, 39–41, 56–57
Hand building, 23, 34
Hazor, 28, 50–52
India, 30
Industry, 13, 15, 17
Iraq, 27–28
Israel, 28, 49–52, 63
Italy, 25–26, 45, 55, 57
Japan, 11, 13, 22–23, 30
Jōmon, 11

Jordan, 49, 62–63
Kaolin, 18, 19, 20, 38
Kilns, 41–42, 46–49, 67
Maya, 31
Mediterranean region, 27, 30, 35, 38–39, 45, 49, 53–54, 57
Mesopotamia, 44
Mexico, 13
Middle East, 13, 30, 32, 35, 38, 45–46, 53–54, 57, 63

Molds, 24–26
Mycenae, 63
Mycenaean III/A, 63
Native Americans, 10, 13–14, 16, 31, 44
Nazca culture, 33
North America, 10, 13
Painting, 10, 17, 31, 36, 38–39, 55–57, 60
Peru, 33, 37, 42, 55
Petrie, Flinders, 61–62

Porcelain, 18, 20
Potsherds, 6, 8,
    12–13, 17, 33,
    49–50, 62
Potter's wheel, 26–35
Prehistoric times,
    6–17, 38, 49
Pueblo Indians, 25
Qin Shihuangdi, 43
Radiocarbon dating,
    63–65
Relative dating, 58–62
Sequence dating, 60–62
Slab method, 24

Slip, 9–10, 14, 16,
    24, 39–42
South America, 13,
    32–33, 37, 55
Stoneware, 20
Syria, 34–35, 57, 63
Techniques, 23–25
  coil construction, 23–
    26, 34–35
  combined methods,
    25, 34–35
  hand building, 23, 34
  molds, 24–26
  potter's wheel, 26–35

Tell al-Amarna, 63
Terra-cotta, 43
Thermo-luminescence
    dating, 64, 67
Throwing, 27
Trade, 53–54, 57
United States, 25, 31
Ur, 27–28

Photo Acknowledgments

p. 2, Meredith Pillon/Greek National Tourist Organization; pp. 7, 54, Minneapolis Public Library and Information Center; pp. 8 (inset), 22 (bottom), Office of the State Archaeologist, University of Iowa; pp. 8 (bottom), 31 (bottom), 33, 37, 44, 45, 55 (bottom), Nelson–Atkins Museum of Art; p. 9 (top), The Burke Museum; pp. 9 (bottom), 12 (top and bottom), 13, 17, 20, 21 (top and bottom), 25 (top and bottom), 28 (top and bottom), 29, 32, 34, 38, 39, 41, 42 (top), 47, 51, 52, 53, 62, 66, 68, 70, Independent Picture Service; p. 10, Tennessee State Museum, from a painting by Carlyle Urello; p. 11, Shashinka Photo Library; p. 14, National Museum of Wales; p. 15, Frederick R. Weisman Art Museum, University of Minnesota, Minneapolis; p. 16, Harvey Caplin; pp. 17 (top), 60, The Bettmann Archive; p. 19 (top), Albion Kaolin Company, United Catalysts, Inc.; p. 19 (bottom), Cedar Heights Clay; pp. 22 (top), 26, 30 (top and bottom), 42 (bottom), Northern Clay Center, by Kathy Raskob/IPS; pp. 23, 35 (top and bottom), 49, Gallery 10, Inc.; pp. 24, 69, College of St. Benedict; p. 27, Andrew Beswick; p. 31 (top), Stuart Rome; pp. 40, 46, Steve Woit; p. 43, William Thompson; p. 48 (top), Rina Swentzell; pp. 48 (bottom), 67, Royal Doulton Ltd.; p. 55 (top), Italian Government Travel Office (ENIT); p. 56, IPS/courtesy of Frederick R. Weisman Art Museum, University of Minnesota, Minneapolis; p. 57, Drs. A. A. M. van der Heyden, Naarden, The Netherlands; p. 59 (top), Minnesota Historical Society; p. 59 (bottom), Bureau of Land Management; p. 61, The Mansell Collection; pp. 64, 65 (bottom), University of Miami, Rosenstiel School of Marine and Atmospheric Science, Tritium Laboratory; p. 65 (top), Herbert Haas; p. 71, Roy Kaufman, National Council of American–Soviet Friendship.

Cover photos: Nelson–Atkins Museum of Art (front) and Northern Clay Center, by Kathy Raskob/IPS (back).